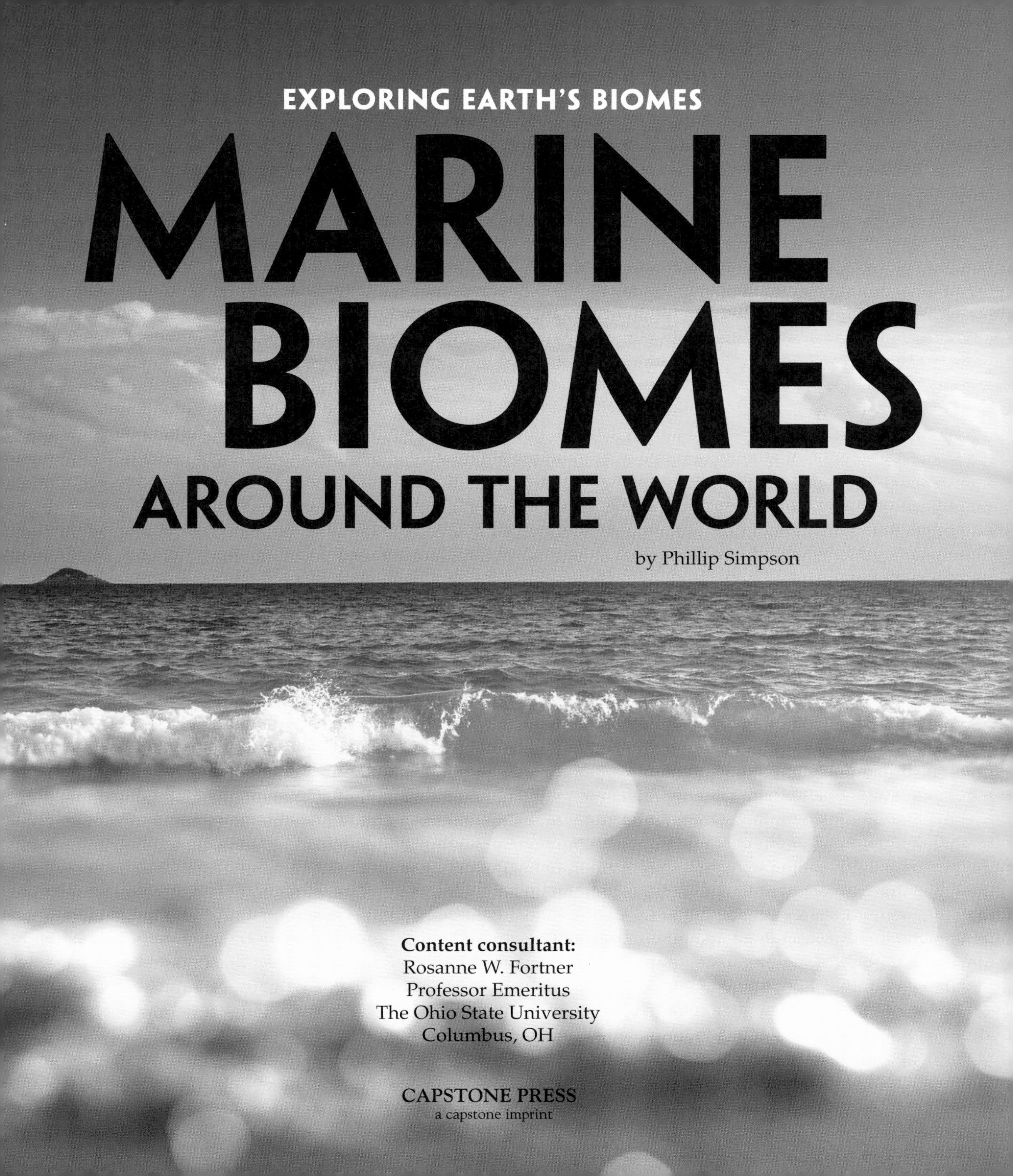

EXPLORING EARTH'S BIOMES

MARINE BIOMES
AROUND THE WORLD

by Phillip Simpson

Content consultant:
Rosanne W. Fortner
Professor Emeritus
The Ohio State University
Columbus, OH

CAPSTONE PRESS
a capstone imprint

Fact Finders Books are published by Capstone Press
1710 Roe Crest Drive, North Mankato, Minnesota 56003
www.capstonepub.com

Library of Congress Cataloging-in-Publication Data
Names: Simpson, Phillip W., 1971–author.
Title: Marine Biomes Around the World / by Phillip Simpson.
Description: North Mankato, Minnesota: Capstone Press, [2020] | Series:
   Fact Finders. Exploring Earth's Biomes | Includes index. | Audience: Age
   8–9. | Audience: Grade 4 to 6.
Identifiers: LCCN 2019002049 | ISBN 9781543572346 (hardcover) | ISBN
   9781543575354 (paperback) | ISBN 9781543572360 (ebook pdf)
Subjects: LCSH: Marine ecology—Juvenile literature.
Classification: LCC QH541.5.S3 S485 2020 | DDC 577.7—dc23
LC record available at https://lccn.loc.gov/2019002049

Editorial Credits
Gina Kammer, editor; Julie Peters, designer; Morgan Walters, media researcher;
Kathy McColley, production specialist

Photo Credits
Alamy: Avalon/Photoshot License, top 13, Doug Perrine, bottom 12; Getty Images:
David Doubilet, bottom 18; Newscom: Credit Paulo de Oliveira/NHPA/Avalon.
red, bottom 26; Science Source: Jessica Wilson, (map) 14; Shutterstock: Achimdiver,
28, Adriana Margarita Larios Arellano, top 22, Andrei Minsk, (maps) 9, Borisoff, (sea)
Cover, Dale Warren, top 7, Damsea, bottom 16, divedog, (seaweed) design element,
Dudarev Mikhail, top 19, fluke samed, bottom 24, HelenField, (earth) bottom 5, Iakov
Kalinin, (beach) design element, khwanchai, bottom 20, Kitnha, (map) middle 5,
Kondratuk Aleksei, bottom 10, Krzysztof Bargiel, (fish) design element, Lickomicko,
(map) 22, Milos Kontic, (diver) Cover, NoPainNoGain, bottom 8, Paul Rawlingson, top
17, PHOTO JUNCTION, (blue water) design element, Pro_Vector, (map) 27, sergemi,
bottom right 4, stihii, bottom 21, superjoseph, middle 15, TierneyMJ, 23, touchoforange,
top 11, Vecton, bottom 6, Vitaly Korovin, (reef) design element, Vladislav Gajic, 29,
vovan, (beach wave) design element, ZoranOrcik, top 25

All internet sites appearing in back matter were available and accurate when this book
was sent to press.

Printed and bound in the USA.
PA70

TABLE OF CONTENTS

CHAPTER 1

THE LARGEST BIOME ON EARTH

Imagine life on Earth without water. An empty, desertlike land stretches out before you. Dead, dry. Could you live in such a world? Probably not.

Today, almost all life on Earth relies on water. Without it, humans wouldn't exist. Throughout our history, people have lived near water. We rely on it for drinking, washing, and watering crops. Water is what the five main biomes—**aquatic**, forest, desert, tundra, and grassland—have in common. Biomes are large zones with a particular type of climate, plants, and animals.

coral reef

aquatic—having to do with water

The two major aquatic biomes are the marine biome and the freshwater biome. The marine biome can be broken down into three types: oceans, coral reefs, and **estuaries**. It's by far the largest biome in the world because it includes the five main oceans: the Pacific, Atlantic, Indian, Arctic, and Southern. The marine biome also includes seas and tidal areas.

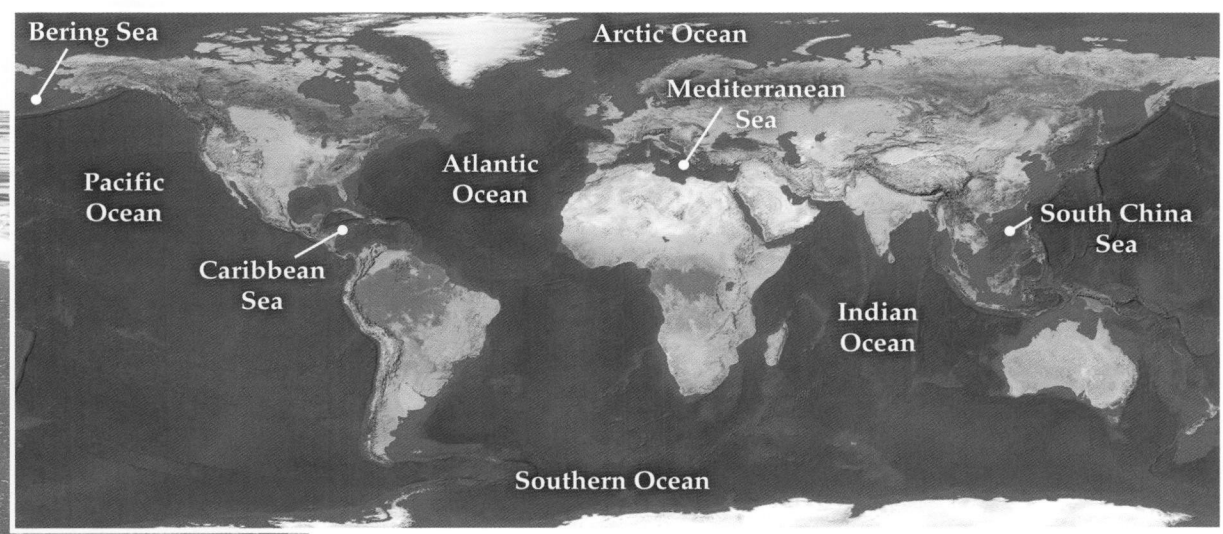

FACT
Water makes up the largest part of Earth, covering more than 70 percent of the planet's surface. From space, Earth looks like a water world.

estuary—the mouth of a large river, where the salt water from an ocean or sea meets the fresh water

The marine biome is different from the freshwater biome because of its water. Marine biome water contains salt. This salt comes from rocks on land that have **eroded** into the oceans and seas. The water later evaporates and returns to land as fresh water. This process is part of the water cycle. All plants and animals on the planet get most of their fresh water from the salt water of the marine biome.

The marine biome provides more than just fresh water. We often think the oxygen we breathe comes mostly from trees. But plants that live in oceans provide much more of Earth's oxygen.

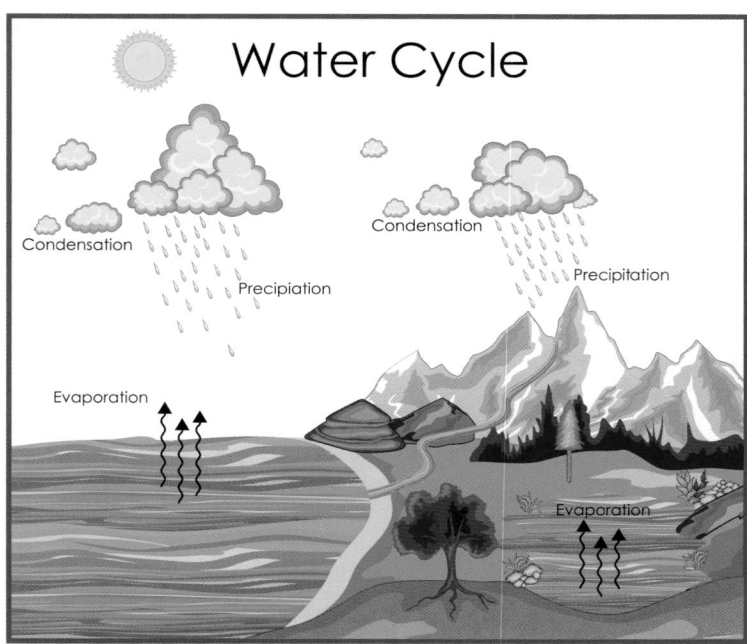

Water Cycle

Condensation

Condensation

Precipiation

Precipitation

Evaporation

Evaporation

Water that evaporates from the ocean is fresh water. It does not include the ocean's salt. Air currents raise the moisture where it condenses into clouds. From the clouds, it falls back to the earth as precipitation, such as in rain or snow. Some of this water flows back to the ocean. The cycle starts over.

erode—to gradually wear away

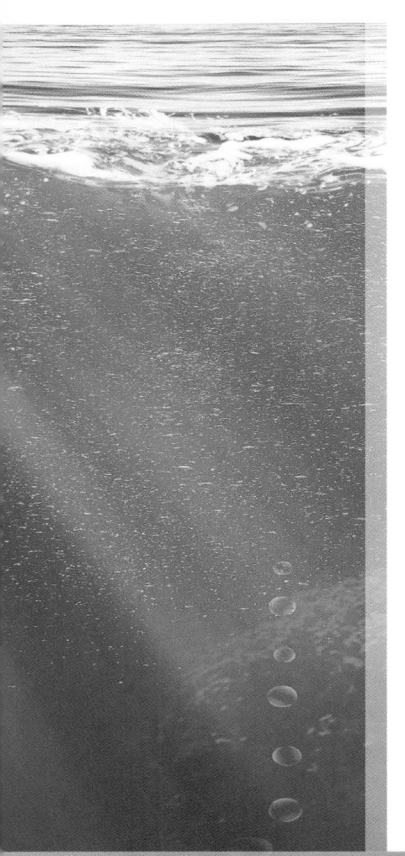

Shrimp and fish were caught by fishermen in Cambodia to sell at market.

Today almost half the world's population lives within 62 miles (100 kilometers) of marine coasts. Why? At first, people moved or migrated in order to be closer to the oceans as a source of food. Later, when trading routes opened up, estuaries and river mouths served as easy ways to transport goods. Ports and harbors provided access for ships to dock and unload and load supplies. The marine biome continues to give people fresh air and water. It also remains a way of transportation and a precious source of food. Seafood is important to many countries for both food and money. Ocean views and seaside activities also attract people to the marine biome.

CHAPTER 2

OCEANS: THE BIG BLUE

Oceans are the largest parts of the marine biome, making up much of Earth's surface. Oceans are so massive and deep that they can be separated into five zones: sunlight, twilight, midnight, the abyss, and the trenches. Each zone has many species. These plants and animals have adapted to their unique environments. The oceans contain the greatest variety of species on the planet.

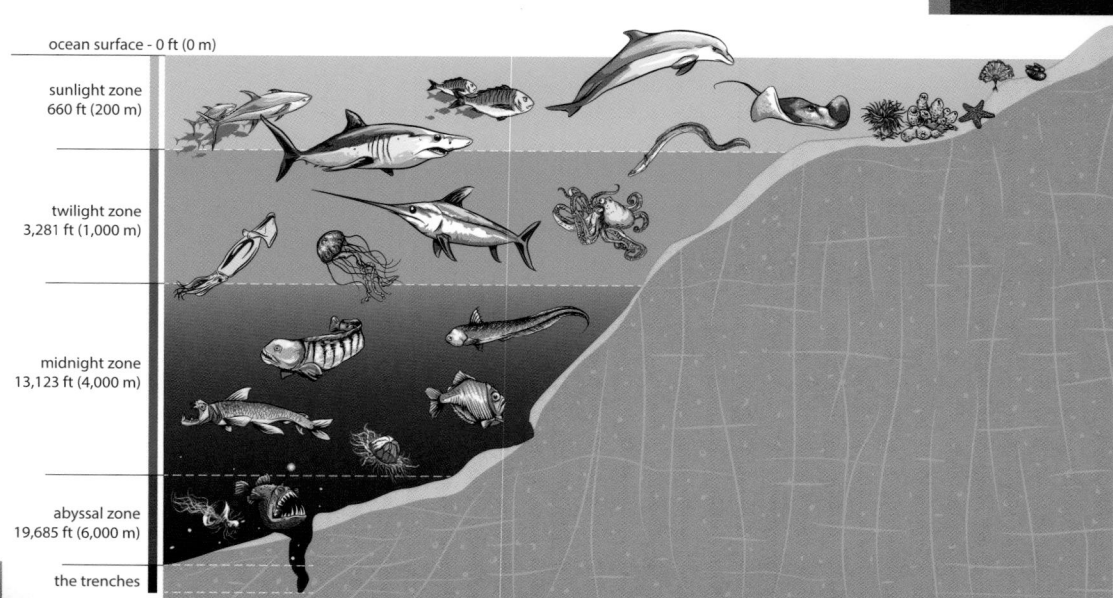

ocean surface - 0 ft (0 m)

sunlight zone
660 ft (200 m)

twilight zone
3,281 ft (1,000 m)

midnight zone
13,123 ft (4,000 m)

abyssal zone
19,685 ft (6,000 m)

the trenches

SUNLIGHT ZONE

The sunlight zone stretches from the ocean's surface to about 660 feet (200 meters) below. This zone has the most light. The light allows marine plants such as seaweed to grow. Many marine animals feed on **phytoplankton** and smaller fish. Most ocean fish, including sharks and rays, live in this zone. The animals have adapted to use their eyes to hunt prey or avoid predators.

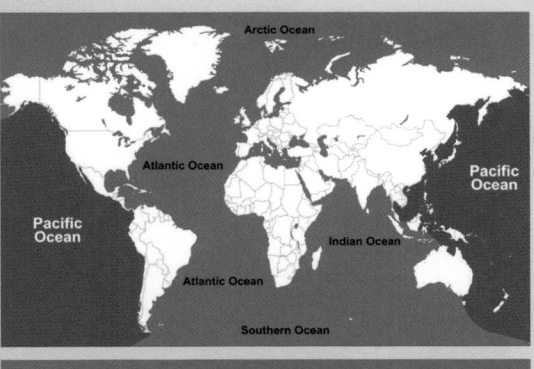

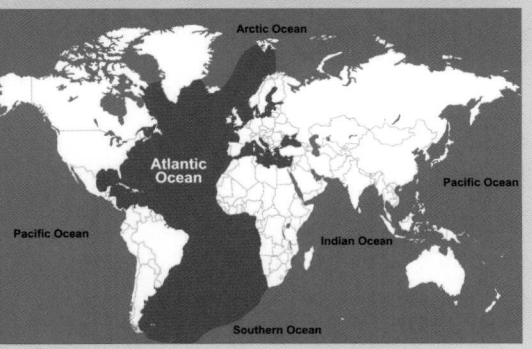

FACT
The Pacific Ocean is the largest ocean in the world. It covers almost one-third of the entire surface of Earth! The Atlantic Ocean is the second-largest ocean. It's a little more than half the size of the Pacific Ocean.

phytoplankton—mostly single-celled plants that live in water and use sunlight and carbon dioxide to make food and oxygen by photosynthesis

TWILIGHT ZONE

The twilight zone is directly below the sunlight zone, reaching down to 3,281 feet (1,000 m). Light is much fainter here than it is above. There is enough light to see during the day but not enough for plants to grow. Larger marine animals such as whales and giant squid dive to these depths to feed on prey. Many fish have large eyes to absorb as much of the dim light as possible. In this zone, some fish glow with **bioluminescence**.

bioluminescence—the production of light by a living organism

giant squid

MIDNIGHT ZONE

The midnight zone descends into darkness up to 13,123 feet (4,000 m). Fish create their own light using their bodies through bioluminescence. The great pressure of the water in this zone would crush an unprotected human. But a squid, for example, can survive because its body contains no air. There are no "gaps" in its body to be crushed. Many fish have soft bodies to survive the water pressure. Their slimy skin has adapted to protect them from the cold. A few have large eyes that are 100 times more sensitive to light than that of a human. Others have no eyes at all. They use senses such as smell to find their way around.

ABYSSAL ZONE

The abyssal zone is deep, dark, and near freezing. There is no light at all, and fewer animals live at these crushing depths up to 19,685 feet (6,000 m). The animals found here are often invertebrates, which have no backbone, such as tiny squid. Their grey or black bodies are an adaptation to the darkness. This camouflage allows them to blend in with their surroundings. Many have large jaws to sift through the sand of the ocean floor. Most of the ocean floor is found in this zone.

Anglerfish can be found in the abyssal zone.

THE TRENCHES

The trenches zone is the deepest part of the ocean below 19,685 feet (6,000 m). The water is near freezing. The weight of the water is the same as 48 Boeing 747 airplanes sitting on you. Despite this, life is still found here. Fish move slowly to conserve energy and need very little oxygen. Soft-shelled **crustaceans** called amphipods live here. They look like large fleas. Trench animals have adaptations much like animals in the zones above, such as having no air in their bodies. Most use bioluminescence to attract food or for disguise.

crustacean—an animal with a hard outer skeleton, including crabs, lobsters, crayfish, shrimp, and barnacles

CHAPTER 3

CORAL REEFS: A SAFE HOME

Coral reefs are part of the marine biome. They form some of the most beautiful places on the planet. Coral reefs are found in warm, shallow water. They often act as barriers to nearby land. They can surround the edges of continents and islands. There are three main types of coral reefs: fringing reefs, barrier reefs, and atolls. Fringing reefs are close to shore and found in shallow water. Barrier reefs are farther out and are in deeper water. Atolls are rings of coral that surround a lagoon. They look like islands.

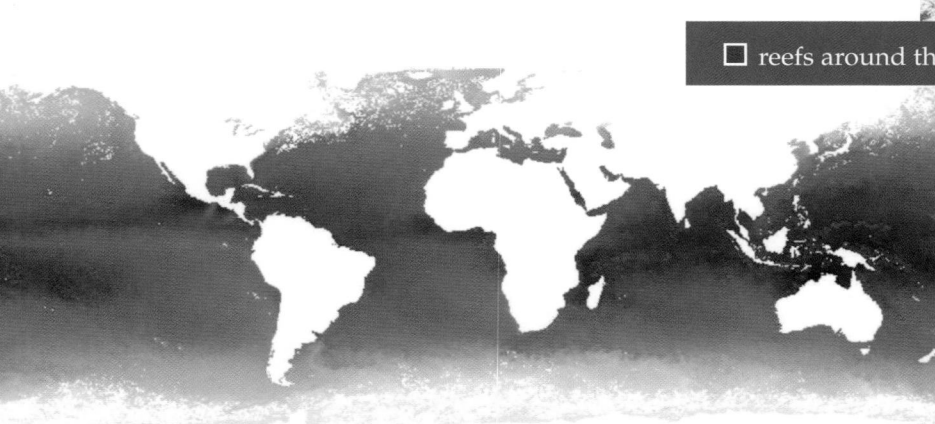

☐ reefs around the world

A coral reef is made from **coral polyps**, which are animals, not plants. When you remove coral from the water, that part is the hard shell of the polyp. A cluster of polyps growing together gives reefs their shape. They provide a home, shelter, and protection for the many sea creatures that live in the reef.

FACT
Large reefs such as the Great Barrier Reef in Australia are between 5,000 and 10,000 years old! That reef is made up of 2,900 smaller reefs. It covers about 1,600 miles (2,575 km), 900 islands, and is one of the most visited reefs in the world.

coral polyp—a tiny organism that has a hard limestone skeleton; the skeletons form the structure of coral reefs

Thousands of sea life species call coral reefs home. These include **microorganisms**, plankton, algae, seaweed, fish, jellyfish, sea anemones, sea urchins, octopus, and starfish. In fact, coral reefs provide homes to almost a quarter of all marine life. Many fish species use coral reefs as nurseries for their young. Animals that live in coral reefs, both predators and their prey, are often masters of camouflage. They have adapted to the region and blend in with the coral, rock, and sand that surround them.

A Suenson's brittle star blends in on a branching fire coral.

Strong waves wear down shores.

The coral reef plays an important role in the survival of our planet. Coral reefs protect shorelines from erosion by acting as barriers to waves and storms. They provide many resources that a marine **ecosystem** needs.

FACT
There are more types of fish in a 2-acre (0.8-hectare) area of coral reef than there are bird species in all of North America!

ecosystem—a system of living and nonliving things in an environment
microorganism—a tiny organism, usually a bacterium, virus, or fungus

17

Coral reefs provide many benefits for humans, such as fish for food. In countries such as Indonesia and Papua New Guinea, fishing villages are often located near coral reefs. Because they rely on the coral reefs for survival, people in these fishing villages have learned to adapt or change with their environment. For example, some villages allow fishing for a few years and then close the fishing grounds for nine months. Others close their coral reefs to fishing most of the time and then do a lot of fishing at once. This helps fish numbers increase and the fish themselves to grow bigger.

A father and son fish in the healthy reefs of Papua New Guinea.

Fishing is an important source of money and food for people on the coasts of Sri Lanka.

Reefs are also important to the worldwide fishing industry. Smaller fish species breed and grow in reefs. They are the food supply for large predator fish such as tuna. People in the worldwide fishing industry hunt these large fish species.

FACT

Coral reefs can help people live longer! Scientists have found that parts of coral reefs can be used to make medicines to treat cancer and other illnesses.

CHAPTER 4

ESTUARIES: A PLACE TO GROW

Estuaries are another type of marine biome. In these places, freshwater streams and rivers meet and mix with the saltwater ocean or sea. Lagoons, river mouths, inlets, and harbors are also estuaries. Some are always open to the sea, but others are flushed with seawater only during storms. Estuaries keep the water clean and clear by filtering the **sediment**. Estuaries are shaped by tides and the weather. Reefs, islands, or areas of mud and sand help protect some estuaries.

aerial view of a river meeting the ocean

These areas of mixed water create a unique ecosystem that is home to many types of animals and plants. Plants such as algae, seaweed, marsh grasses, and mangrove trees grow well in estuaries. Animals living here include worms, oysters, crabs, and water birds. Other species pass through estuaries during their migrations. A good example is the salmon, which migrates from the sea to rivers to lay its eggs. Once born, the young fish migrate back to the sea. Many **migratory** birds use estuaries to rest and eat before continuing their journeys.

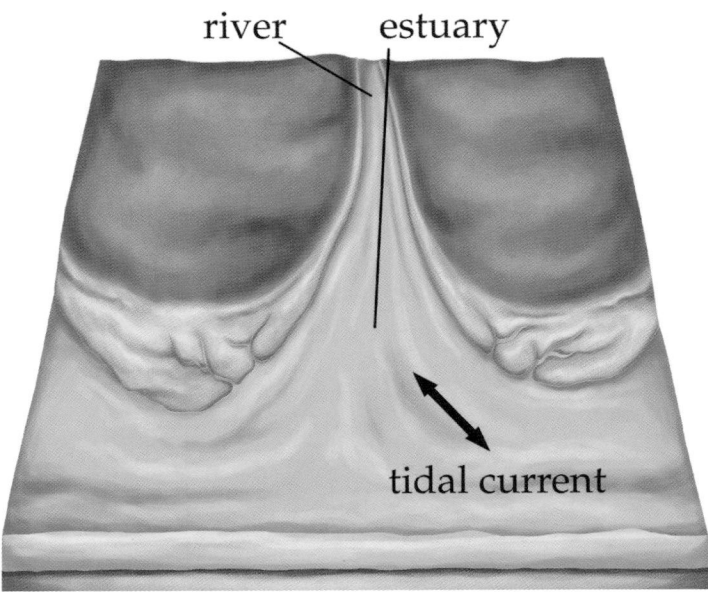

river   estuary

tidal current

migratory—having a way of life including regular travel, such as animals that usually move great distances to find food sources
sediment—sand, mud, and other particles produced from weathering

Animals living in estuaries are also important sources of food for humans. People harvest shellfish such as mussels, oysters, crabs, and shrimp. Bottom-feeding fish such as flounder are common.

Men fish with a net in an estuary in Mexico.

Estimated Population - 2014
- 0 - 40,000
- 40,001 - 80,000
- 80,001 - 120,000
- 120,001 - 160,000
- 160,001 - 200,000
- 200,001 - 240,000
- 240,001 - 280,000
- > 280,000

The Chesapeake Bay on the East Coast is the largest estuary in the United States. Over 18.2 million people live in the region.

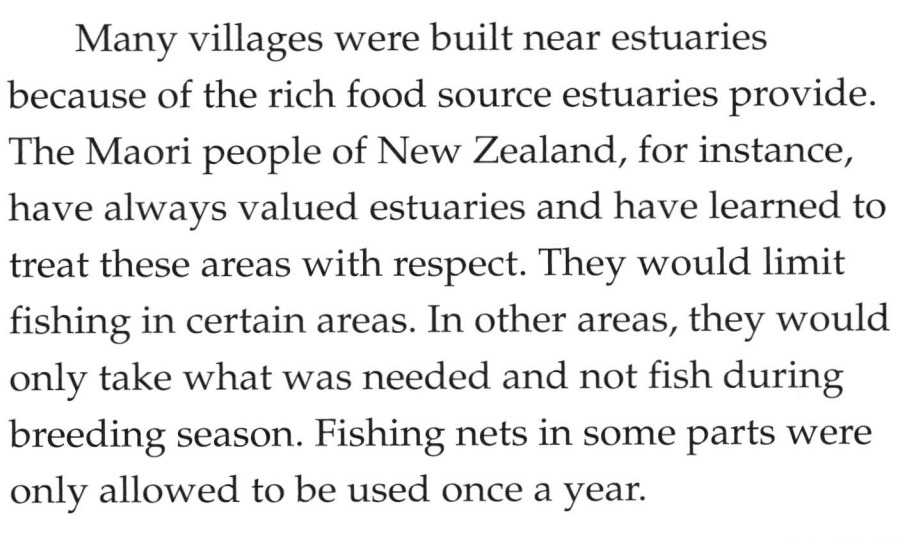

Many villages were built near estuaries because of the rich food source estuaries provide. The Maori people of New Zealand, for instance, have always valued estuaries and have learned to treat these areas with respect. They would limit fishing in certain areas. In other areas, they would only take what was needed and not fish during breeding season. Fishing nets in some parts were only allowed to be used once a year.

New York City is located on the Hudson River Estuary.

FACT
Towns or cities are usually located near estuaries because of the abundant food supply. Estuaries provide ways to transport goods and people. However, this function also puts estuaries at risk from pollution such as sewage and waste.

CHAPTER 5

HUMANS AND WATER

While people greatly value and benefit from the marine biome, they also are the biome's greatest threat. By polluting and overfishing the marine biome, humans have affected every part of this complex ecosystem.

Oil is one of our most used and useful energy resources. However, locating and extracting oil creates some risks for the marine biome. Oil is often located below the sea floor. During an oil spill or accident, sea creatures either become covered in oil or swallow it. Oil also affects the food chain by **contaminating** all food sources. This contamination affects humans as well, because many people rely on seafood for survival.

Crabs on a beach are covered in oil.

A fisherman pulls fish out of the water with a net.

Fishing in developed countries has had a severe impact on the marine biome. Fish numbers have halved since 1970 and are now the lowest they've ever been. Numbers of some types of fish have decreased by 75 percent. In addition to overfishing, modern fishing methods can harm the biome. Massive fishing boats drag huge fishing nets behind them. The boats and nets damage and destroy marine habitats on the sea floor.

FACT
In some countries, people aren't as harmful to the marine environment. They use simple fishing lines and nets to catch enough food to eat and some to sell. Their impact is small.

contaminate—to make dirty or unfit for use, such as in the pollution or poisoning of an animal or area

25

Human garbage is also incredibly harmful to the marine biome. People often dump plastic items, especially bags and bottles, into the ocean. A sea animal may mistake this floating trash for food and eat it. The plastic can choke the animal and cause the animal to suffocate. A sea animal can also get stuck in plastic rings, which chokes the animal or shortens its life.

Fish, such as the Titan triggerfish, will eat plastic garbage thinking it is food.

Dumping sewage and industrial waste into the marine biome harms the entire ecosystem. In addition, fish and other marine animals eat such waste and then pass it along the food chain. Remember that the food chain includes humans. This means we could end up eating our own waste! Yuck!

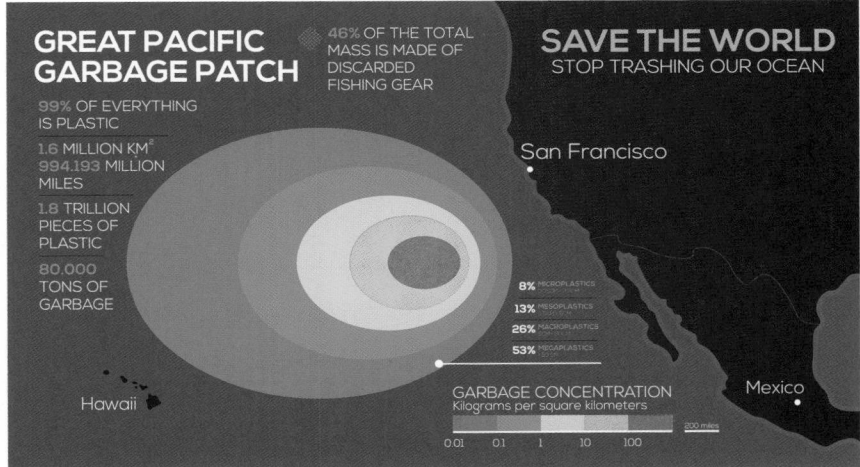

GREAT PACIFIC GARBAGE PATCH

46% OF THE TOTAL MASS IS MADE OF DISCARDED FISHING GEAR

SAVE THE WORLD
STOP TRASHING OUR OCEAN

99% OF EVERYTHING IS PLASTIC

1.6 MILLION KM²
994.193 MILLION MILES

1.8 TRILLION PIECES OF PLASTIC

80,000 TONS OF GARBAGE

San Francisco

8% MICROPLASTICS
13% MESOPLASTICS
26% MACROPLASTICS
53% MEGAPLASTICS

Mexico

Hawaii

GARBAGE CONCENTRATION
Kilograms per square kilometers

200 miles

0.01   0.1   1   10   100

FACT

More than 1 million tons (.9 metric ton) of plastic enters the ocean each year from rivers. The Pacific Ocean contains a floating island of plastic called the Great Pacific Garbage Patch, or GPGP. Located between Hawaii and California, it's the largest mass of ocean plastic in the world. Being made of plastic, it floats rather than sinks. The GPGP covers an area three times the size of France!

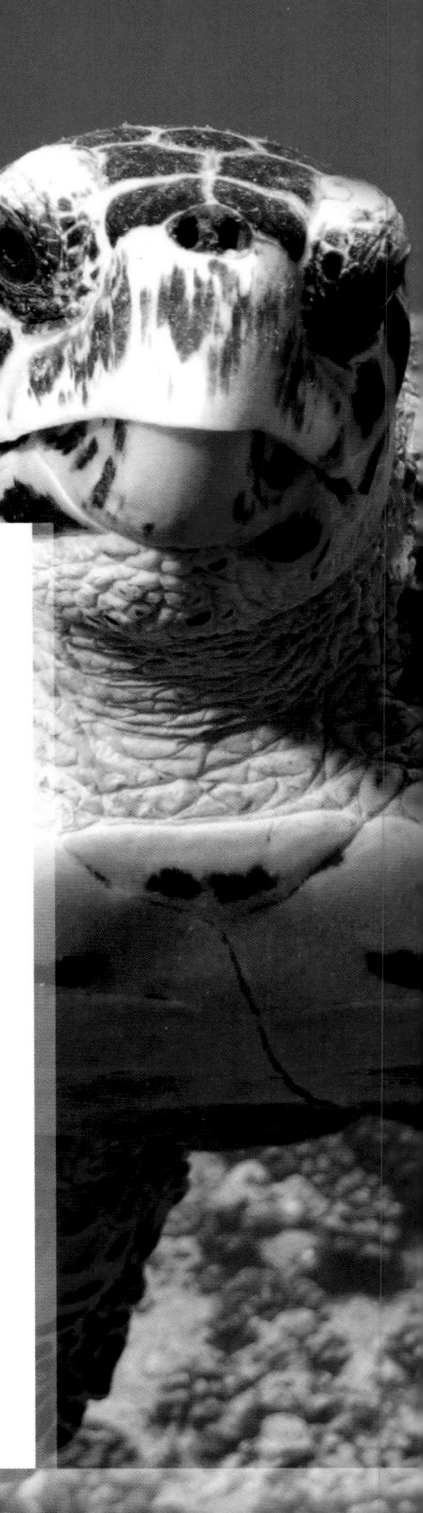

CHAPTER 6

THE MARINE BIOME OF THE FUTURE

The marine biome has everything humans need to survive. People depend on the marine biome for food, air, and water, and sometimes as a source of income. That's why so many people live near the marine biome and why it's important to look after it. Examples set by people in Indonesia, Papua New Guinea, and New Zealand show ways to live in better harmony with the marine biome. Countries such as the Philippines have set smaller catch limits and try to avoid catching animals like turtles and young fish. They've created protected areas for marine animals. These examples show that we can still use marine resources respectfully and carefully.

For the marine biome to survive, problems such as overfishing and polluting need to be addressed. We can protect marine habitats by creating marine reserves and using more environmentally friendly fishing practices. By working together, we can preserve the marine biome for future generations.

fish farm

WHAT CAN YOU DO?

Consider donating to organizations that protect and preserve the marine biome. Check cans of seafood and only buy farmed fish. Recycle items that you can and dispose of other garbage responsibly.

GLOSSARY

aquatic (uh-KWAH-tik)—having to do with water

bioluminescence (BUY-oh-loo-men-e-senss)—the production of light by a living organism

contaminate (kuhn-TA-muh-nayt)—to make dirty or unfit for use, such as the pollution or poisoning of an animal or area

coral polyp (KOR-uhl POL-ip)—a tiny organism that has a hard limestone skeleton; the skeletons form the structure of coral reefs

crustacean (kruhss-TAY-shuhn)—an animal with a hard outer skeleton, including crabs, lobsters, crayfish, shrimp, and barnacles

ecosystem (EE-koh-sis-tuhm)—a system of living and nonliving things in an environment

erode (i-ROHD)—to gradually wear away

estuary (ESS-chu-er-ee)—the mouth of a large river, where the salt water from an ocean or sea meets fresh water

microorganism (MYE-kro-OR-gan-iz-um)—a tiny organism, usually a bacterium, virus, or fungus

migratory (MYE-ghruh-tohr-ee)—having a way of life including regular travel, such as animals that usually move great distances to find food sources

phytoplankton (FITE-oh-plangk-tuhn)—mostly single-celled plants that live in water and use sunlight and carbon dioxide to make food and oxygen by photosynthesis

sediment (SED-uh-muhnt)—sand, mud, and other particles produced from weathering

READ MORE

Gagne, Tammy. *Marine Ecosystems*. Earth's Ecosystems. Mankato, MN: 12 Story Library, 2018.

Hansen, Grace. *Marine Biome*. Biomes. Minneapolis: Abdo Kids, 2017.

Spilsbury, Louise, and Richard Spilsbury. *Marine Biomes*. Earth's Natural Biomes. New York: Crabtree Publishing Company, 2018.

Sullivan, Laura L. *24 Hours in the Ocean*. A Day in an Ecosystem. New York: Cavendish Square, 2018.

INTERNET SITES

Marine Biome
https://www.eartheclipse.com/ecosystem/marine-biome.html

The Marine Biome
http://www.ucmp.berkeley.edu/exhibits/biomes/marine.php

World Biomes: Marine
http://kids.nceas.ucsb.edu/biomes/marine.html

CRITICAL THINKING QUESTIONS

1. Why is the marine biome so important? If humans destroy the marine biome, what would be the effects on Earth?
2. Name two benefits of coral reefs.
3. What are the five ocean zones? How have plants and animals adapted to live in them?
4. What are some things humans can do to help preserve the marine biome? What can you do at home to help?

INDEX